SELF-CONFIDENCE

FORMULA

NAPOLEON HILL

SELF-CONFIDENCE

FORMULA

YOUR GUIDE TO SELF-RELIANCE AND SUCCESS

Published and distributed by:

SOUND WISDOM
P.O. Box 310
Shippensburg, PA 17257-0310

717-530-2122

info@soundwisdom.com

www.soundwisdom.com

ISBN 13 TP: 978-1-64095-234-8

ISBN 13 eBook: 978-1-64095-235-5

For Worldwide Distribution, Printed in the U.S.A.

2 3 4 5 6 7 8 / 25 24 23 22 21

You are now in possession of the great Pass Key that will unlock the door to whatever you wish yourself to be. Call this great key whatever you wish. Consider it in the light of a purely scientific force if you choose; or, look upon it as a Divine power, belonging to the great mass of unknown phenomena which mankind has not yet fathomed. The result in either case will be the same, SUCCESS!

—**Napoleon Hill,** "Self-Confidence,"
from the Applied Psychology course
at George Washington Institute, 1917

CONTENTS

PREFACE

Man is timid and apologetic; he is no longer upright; he dares not say, "I think," "I am," but quotes some saint or sage.

—**Ralph Waldo Emerson, "Self-Reliance"**

WHAT is the most crucial trait for determining an individual's success in life?

- Desire?
- Definiteness of purpose?
- Faith?
- A positive mental attitude?

What if there were a quality whose presence energized all these other success requisites—and whose absence rendered them innocuous?

According to Napoleon Hill, there is such a foundational attribute, one that both contributes to and results from all principles of individual achievement that came to form his Law of Success philosophy. As he exclaims:

> Try as hard as you wish and you cannot be happy unless you BELIEVE IN YOURSELF! Work with all the strength at your command and you cannot accumulate more than barely enough to live on unless you BELIEVE IN YOURSELF!
>
> The one and only person in all this world through whose efforts you can be supremely happy UNDER ALL CIRCUMSTANCES, and through whose labor you can accumulate all the material wealth that you can use legitimately, is YOURSELF![1]

Self-confidence might rightly be understood as the backbone of Hill's success system. But despite how crucial it is for prosperity and happiness, this characteristic is significantly underdeveloped in most individuals.

The majority of human beings in today's world move through life aimlessly and dejectedly, casting their eyes on the ground rather than up and ahead to the financial, spiritual, and emotional riches they could claim. They allow external opinions to dictate how they see themselves and how they see the world. Their passivity permits negative thoughts to infiltrate their subconscious mind, which then undermines them by working to translate those dominating ideas into reality. As a result, people without self-confidence *drift* through life, endlessly dissatisfied with their circumstances and using this unrest as an alibi for their poor self-regard.

The time for self-doubt and self-criticism is over. Your faith in yourself and your ability to attain your chief desire make the difference between your success and failure. Hanging in the balance are your emotional and financial security. Today—*this very minute*—you begin a journey of discovering, acknowledging, and sharing your strengths so that you can regain the energy and motivation you need to achieve your goals.

> The time for self-doubt and self-criticism is over.

This book equips you with the strategies recommended by Hill for controlling your thoughts in order to boost self-confidence. After reading it, you will not only be able to operate at a higher plane of thought and action—attracting more opportunities, gaining influence, and enjoying better relationships—but you will also be able to instill this critical quality in others, especially younger individuals, who are currently forming their sense of self.

OVERCOMING THE DEVIL OF SELF-DOUBT

A small-town reporter from Wise County, Virginia, Hill knew the impact that self-confidence had on one's trajectory in life. It was self-confidence, inspired in him by his stepmother, that enabled him to pursue a dream that raised him out of the poverty of his childhood. Chancing upon an interview with Andrew Carnegie, Hill received instructions from the steel magnate to undertake a research project to which Hill would end up dedicating his life: studying the thoughts, attitudes, and behaviors of the most successful individuals in order to produce a comprehensive philosophy of success.

Decades of initial research contributed to Hill's Law of Success philosophy, which he would elaborate in countless speeches, magazine articles, books, and study programs. From his eight-volume series *The Law of Success*, to his all-time bestseller *Think and Grow Rich*, to *Napoleon Hill's Golden Rule Magazine*, to the *PMA: Science of Success* course, and beyond—all of Hill's writings share the goal of elevating people's thoughts so that they can reach the heights of success, however they define that for themselves.

But as Hill recognized from firsthand experience, without self-confidence humans cannot harness the power of their thoughts to attain their chief desire. After decades of research and teaching his success philosophy, Hill discovered that his own poor self-regard was inhibiting his freedom of thought and preventing him from bringing his dreams to fruition. He shares:

> Out of my difficulties, which were burdensome enough up to this point, grew another which seemed more painful than all the others combined. It was the realization that I had spent the better portion of my past years in chasing a rainbow, searching hither and yon for the cause of success, and finding myself now more helpless than any of the 25,000 people whom I had judged as being "failures."
>
> This thought was almost maddening. Moreover, it was extremely humiliating, because I had been lecturing all over the country, in schools and colleges and before business organizations, presuming to tell other people how to apply the seventeen principles of success, while here I was, unable to apply them myself. I was sure that I never could again face the world with a feeling of confidence.
>
> Every time I looked at myself in a mirror I noticed an expression of self-contempt on my face, and not infrequently I did say things to the man in the

mirror which are not printable. I had begun to place myself in the category of charlatans who offer others a remedy for failure which they themselves cannot successfully apply.[2]

Overcoming negative self-perceptions caused by fear and the destructive attitudes ingrained in him by society was the hardest work of Hill's life, but it was also the most rewarding. Once he was able to wrest himself from the clutches of fear and self-doubt, he found himself able to enact his success philosophy to its fullest extent, becoming the foremost expert on personal achievement.

THE FIRST SUCCESS REQUISITE

Because it is crucial for controlling one's thoughts, organizing them into definite plans, and ultimately taking action on them, self-confidence is one of the most important factors influencing personal success. To those well-versed in Hill's success philosophy, this might seem questionable. After all, "self-confidence" is not one of the original 17 principles of individual achievement presented in *The Law of Success*, nor is it one of the 13 steps to riches detailed in *Think and Grow Rich*. However, it was the primary success requisite identified by Hill in his early speeches on what he then called "Applied Psychology."

Teaching a course at the George Washington Institute in Chicago in 1917, Hill shared a lesson that emerged out of his interview with Carnegie, in which the great industrialist declared, "With a strong sense of self-worth, no amount of poverty can keep one from success. Confidence is a state of mind, necessary to succeed, and the starting point of developing self-confidence is definiteness of purpose."[3] Hill's experience proved Carnegie's words to be true, for his initial research revealed that

> the difference between the man who achieves success and the man who does not is not necessarily in brain capacity. More often the difference is in the use men make of their latent ability.... Usually the man who develops and uses all of his latent powers is a man who has plenty of self-confidence.[4]

He further shares that "a careful analysis of the successful men of the world shows that the dominating quality which they all possessed was SELF-CONFIDENCE."[5] Because it must be present to control one's thought impulses and translate motivation into action, Hill names self-confidence as the key differentiator between success and failure.

The absence of self-confidence, on the other hand, allows negative thought impulses access to the subconscious mind, which then actively works against one's desire for success. As Hill reports in a January 1922 magazine article, "We have learned that men are limited only by their own lack of self-confidence and faith in their fellowmen."[6] He further notes that although self-confidence "is an essential quality for all worthwhile accomplishments...it is the quality in which most of us are weakest—not a weakness that many of us acknowledge, but it exists just the same."[7] His research revealed that a remarkable 90 percent of the people he analyzed lacked self-confidence, regardless of how physically or mentally capable they were. Even those who practiced Hill's success system struggled with self-criticism, severely limiting the efficacy of the program. Hill laments that:

> The same intelligence that declares itself in complete harmony with this philosophy, goes on too often in the self-same way with its criticisms of self, thereby proving that it has never taken the lesson home. In short, the great mass of humanity seems to be content to be tossed about with the driftwood of thought, rather than to make the necessary effort to assert the "I" and know its divine power.[8]

The next chapter explores why self-doubt and insecurity are the dominant states in which humanity operates in the present day. But for now, suffice it to say that a lack of self-confidence is one of the greatest maladies of today's world, one that is responsible for the rampant helplessness, lack of self-control, procrastination, and despair that characterize modern society.

Given its impact on individual achievement, why, then, does Hill not name self-confidence as one of the core success principles? Don M. Green, executive director and CEO of the Napoleon Hill Foundation, provides a clue when he notes that Hill later subsumed self-confidence under the broader category of enthusiasm, which Hill originally designated as the second requisite for success.[9] Certainly, self-confidence drives enthusiasm, but it is tied to the other principles as well. For example, Hill's five-step formula for using autosuggestion to increase faith is called the "Self-Confidence Formula."[10] That is because self-confidence is both the input and the output in Hill's success system: you must build your faith in yourself (input) to become more self-reliant and successful (output). Put another way: "In order to become an active participant in the Philosophy of Success, you must first possess the proper mental attitude that is conducive to utilizing the other remaining principles of achievement"[11]—a positive mental attitude to be sure, but one directed largely toward yourself, your capability, and the riches that are awaiting your appropriation.

The first requisite for success in Hill's original achievement philosophy and the culmination of one's efforts to obtain riches, self-confidence is a critical ingredient in a successful, fulfilling life. As Hill informed his students at the George Washington

Institute, "You will never enjoy greater happiness than that which you will experience through the development of Self-Confidence."[12] Those who lack it must work diligently to cultivate it, or they risk spending their entire life drifting and dissatisfied. The 10 percent who possess it must protect themselves from internal and external influences that threaten to undermine it. In the words of Emerson, one "should learn to detect and watch that gleam of light which flashes across his mind from within, more than the luster of the firmament of bards and sages."[13]

Whatever your reason for reading this book, you will discover immediate benefit from the application of its principles. Note that you will undoubtedly find your progress magnified by working through this content in the setting of a book club or study group, wherein the mastermind principle can be applied to reach higher-level orders of thinking. When you commit yourself to practicing the steps outlined in this book, you will surely open yourself up to great personal growth and momentum toward achieving your dreams.

KEY POINTS

🔑 To heighten your success, you must elevate your thoughts—especially the thoughts you think about yourself.

🔑 Self-confidence holds the key to attracting more opportunities, gaining influence, enjoying better relationships, and experiencing greater peace of mind.

🔑 Although 90 percent of individuals lack this essential success ingredient, people might not be aware of it because they incorrectly assume poor self-worth is the only symptom. Other symptoms can include:

✓ burnout

✓ dissatisfaction

✓ erratic behavior

✓ procrastination

✓ aimlessness

✓ passivity

🔑 As the first requisite for success, self-confidence is the backbone of Hill's success philosophy. Hill eventually grouped it with *enthusiasm*, but it is tied to all the principles of individual achievement.

Personal growth and momentum toward achievement will be yours when you...

CULTIVATE A STATE OF MIND
TO COMMIT TO GROWTH

Check yourself against the list of symptoms of low self-confidence provided in the Key Points above. From which of these do you currently suffer? Are you experiencing any other symptoms that might be related to low self-confidence? Take some time to journal about any relationship you can identify between your actions, experiences, and sense of self. Did any connections surprise you?

The time for self-doubt and self-criticism is over. You are worthy of happiness and success. Looking at your reflection in the mirror, point your finger at the person you see, and tell them—out loud—that they are capable and deserving of prosperity and joy.

Share the results of your self-examination in the context of a study group. Encourage members to share about how a lack of self-confidence might be limiting their potential and holding them back from attaining their chief desire. Commit as a group to working through the concepts and strategies detailed in this book to magnify everyone's results.

CHAPTER 1

WHAT IS SELF-CONFIDENCE?

A man without self-confidence is like a ship without a rudder: he wastes his time without moving in the right direction.

—**Napoleon Hill,**
"What I Learned from
Analyzing Ten Thousand People"

SELF-CONFIDENCE is much more than a quality or trait; it is a state of mind. Hill provides an illuminating definition:

> What is self-confidence? I will tell you what it is: it is the little glass window through which you may look and see the real manpower within your body. Self-confidence is self-discovery—finding out who you are and what you can do. It is the banishment of fear. It is the acquirement of mental courage. It is the turning on of the light of human intelligence through the use of common sense.[14]

Self-confidence is not vanity or the byproduct of an inflated ego. It is the lens through which we can see ourselves for *who we really are*: incredible, capable human beings with unlimited potential for greatness.

While our vision is often clouded by the darkness of our doubts, fears, and self-criticisms, we should not mistake this muddled view with reality. Wiping away the grime that the world has deposited onto our sense of self, we must learn to ground our thoughts in faith so that we can make meaningful progress on our success journey and enjoy the freedom that peace of mind brings. We are called to engage in the deep work of self-discovery to build our self-worth, identifying our individual gifts and determining how we can use them to better the lives of ourselves and others.

> Self-confidence is much more than a quality or trait; it is a state of mind.

Once we recognize that, in our thoughts, we already possess invaluable, inexhaustible resources for translating our dreams into reality, we can cultivate a mental fortitude that ensures adversity will not derail us from attaining our definite chief aim.

"

If you possess self-confidence, many things naturally work in your favor. Believing in yourself and your ability to succeed at whatever you put your mind to is a priceless asset that cannot be purchased at any cost. Knowing that you have an innate 'can-do' attitude prevents you from accepting failure as either part of your genetic makeup or your destiny.[15]

"

As Hill suggests, self-confidence is a "can-do" attitude that leverages enthusiasm, faith, and a positive mental attitude to support personal initiative. It is the mindset through which we find the seeds of opportunity within even the most difficult times. With self-confidence,

> you will accomplish more BECAUSE YOU WILL DARE TO UNDERTAKE MORE! You will realize, possibly for the first time in your life, that you possess the ability to accomplish anything that YOU WISH TO ACCOMPLISH! You will realize how little your success in any undertaking will depend upon others and how much it will depend upon YOU![16]

When you recognize that you are not powerless to change your circumstances—that regardless of your material resources, you have a priceless asset in your thoughts that can be directed toward achieving exactly what you want in life—your motivation and your ability to accomplish more in life will greatly improve. To paraphrase William Ernest Henley, you will realize that you—not anyone or anything else—are the master of your fate and the captain of your soul.[17] In his essay "Self-Reliance," Emerson offers similar advice:

"

Trust thyself: every heart vibrates to that iron string. Accept the place the divine providence has for you, the society of your contemporaries, the connection of events. Great men have always done so, and confided themselves childlike to the genius of their age, betraying their perception that the absolutely trustworthy was seated at their heart, working through their hands, predominating in all their being. And we are now men, and must accept in the highest mind the same transcendent destiny; and not minors and invalids in a protected corner, not cowards fleeing before a revolution, but guides, redeemers, and benefactors, obeying the Almighty effort, and advancing on Chaos and the Dark.[18]

"

Your transcendent destiny awaits you, but you must learn to value and trust yourself in order to boldly take action on your definite major purpose—that iron string which vibrates deep within you, structuring your desires, interests, and goals. Your power in life derives from your sense of self—your appreciation of your unique capabilities and your efforts to develop them by living in alignment with your major purpose. Accordingly, when you engage in self-criticism or avoid self-examination altogether, you relinquish your power over chaos and failure.

THE ENEMIES TO SELF-CONFIDENCE

Emerson's musical imagery in the quotation above enables us to appreciate the physical dimensions of Hill's success philosophy. Explaining that our thoughts are made of vibrations that, although invisible, create change in the material world, Hill stresses the importance of directing those thoughts to constructive ends. As he theorizes, "the ether is filled with a form of universal power which adapts itself to the nature of the thoughts we hold in our minds; and influences us, in natural ways, to transmute our thoughts into their physical equivalent."[19] Just like the string on an instrument vibrates according to how it has been tuned, humans' thought impulses are vibrations whose frequency depends on the pitch to which they've been tuned. If our thought impulses are tuned to negative pitches, such as limiting beliefs and fears, then they will harmonize with other negative energies in the atmosphere. On the other hand, when our thoughts align with the iron string of our definite major purpose and are focused on the certainty of our success, then we experience the euphony of productive resonance.

For most individuals, a lack of self-confidence prevents us from leveraging the power of our thought impulses. This poor self-worth results from three interrelated elements: worry, hopelessness, and fear. At the root of these mental states is the programming we receive from our environment. As Emerson says, "Society everywhere is in conspiracy against the manhood of every one of its members."[20] Put another way: society does not support the maturation of individuals because it does not encourage freedom of thought or independence in action. Instead of motivating men and women to act boldly on their definite chief aim, it renders them passive and aimless. Hill underscores this unfortunate reality when he declares:

> The great curse of the age is FEAR or LACK OF SELF-CONFIDENCE! With this evil removed... you will see yourself rapidly transforming into a person of STRENGTH and INITIATIVE! You will see yourself breaking the ranks of that great mass which we call FOLLOWERS, in which you have been floating, and moving up into the front row of that select few which we call LEADERS! LEADERSHIP ONLY COMES THROUGH SUPREME BELIEF IN SELF, AND YOU NOW KNOW HOW TO DEVELOP THAT BELIEF![21]

Fear inspires passivity and diminishes personal initiative. When this passivity grants the negative influences from our environment access to our subconscious mind, we find ourselves swept along a current that moves us increasingly further away from our definite major purpose. Hill asks:

"

What strange fear is it that gets into the minds of men and short-circuits their approach to this secret power from within, and when it is recognized and used lifts men to great heights of achievement? How and why do the vast majority of the people of the world become the victims of a hypnotic rhythm which destroys their capacity to use the secret power of their own minds? How can this rhythm be broken?[22]

"

Cosmic Habitforce, the natural principle referred to in these lines, can work either for good or for bad depending on whether the thoughts it replicates are constructive or destructive. Our vulnerability to others' negativity and misguided ideas effects the same results as hypnosis: we become lulled into a state of helplessness and self-destructive behavior, which in turn allows destructive thoughts to embed themselves into our subconscious mind and work in tandem with it to become reality. Because hypnotic rhythm, when misused, strengthens our failure consciousness and undermines our self-confidence, Hill enjoins us to "keep

FEAR away from your conscious mind as you would keep poison out of your food, for it is the one barrier that will stand between you and Self-Confidence."[23]

Two of Hill's "six basic fears" are particularly detrimental to self-confidence: the fear of poverty and the fear of criticism.[24] That is because in addition to being a state of mind, self-confidence is a muscle: we strengthen it through exercise, which comes in the form of active faith in our abilities, our values, and our plans. When we allow fear to direct our thoughts, our self-confidence muscle atrophies. Fearing failure and rejection, we avoid countering dominant opinions or taking actions that might "rock the boat." We permit others to control how we perceive ourselves and the world around us.

Fear and worry also prevent us from recognizing that "every failure brings with it the seed of an equivalent success."[25] When our state of mind is one of fear and worry, we give failure power over our future rather than using it as a catalyst for growth and progress. To be sure, failure "breaks down one's morale, destroys self-confidence, subdues enthusiasm, dulls imagination, and drives away definitenes of purpose."[26] However, the majority of experiences we perceive as failure are only temporary defeat disguised as failure; we cement defeat as failure when we accept it. Viewing adversity as opportunity rather than defeat enables us to build our resilience, self-reliance, and thus self-confidence. By destroying our faith, fear and worry cause us to sink into hopelessness.

Giving in to the negative influences in our environment— allowing them to take root in our mind and diminish our sense of self—not only causes us to accept temporary defeat as final, but it also destroys our ability to make decisions and take action to create positive change in our life. "All decisions require courage," or the self-confidence in one's abilities to handle the consequences of our choices.[27] Indecision is the general state of humanity, which is why so few live out all the dreams they have for themselves. In order to build self-confidence, as we will discover in the rest of the book, we must take decisive action.

You are now on the journey to confident, purposeful living. With the support of the principles described in ensuing chapters, you will find assurance in the power of your definite chief aim and the tools to create a mindset primed to identify and accept the opportunities awaiting you.

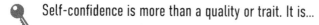

KEY POINTS

🔑 Self-confidence is more than a quality or trait. It is...

   ✓ a state of mind—one through which we find opportunity

   ✓ a "can-do" attitude that supports personal initiative

   ✓ a muscle that has to be exercised to maintain its strength

   ✓ the iron string to which your authentic self vibrates

🔑 When we tune into negative channels of thought, we step out of alignment with our definite major purpose.

🔑 Self-confidence is diminished by worry, hopelessness, and fear—particularly the fear of criticism and the fear of poverty. Fearing rejection and failure, we allow others to control how we perceive ourselves and the world around us.

🔑 Viewing adversity as opportunity rather than failure enables us to build our resilience, self-reliance, and thus self-confidence.

🔑 Confident, purposeful living will be yours when you...

CULTIVATE A STATE OF MIND
TO OVERCOME FEAR

Take some time to explore the following questions: What is your definite major purpose? What is that iron string to which your entire being vibrates? Are you currently living in alignment with it? If not, into what thought impulses are you currently tuned? Journal about two changes you could make in your life right now to connect more deeply with your definite major purpose.

Fear is a negative emotion that is more detrimental to your self-confidence than any other. Make a habit of applying positive emotions to your thoughts so that there is no room in your mind for fear, for as Hill notes, "Positive and negative emotions cannot occupy the mind at the same time."[28] Apply the following emotions to thoughts—spoken out loud—affirming your ability to attain your definite major purpose:

✓ desire

✓ faith

✓ love

✓ sex

✓ enthusiasm

✓ romance

✓ hope

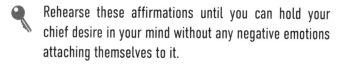 Rehearse these affirmations until you can hold your chief desire in your mind without any negative emotions attaching themselves to it.

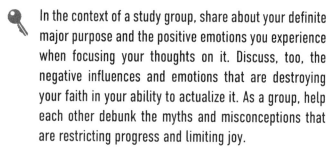 In the context of a study group, share about your definite major purpose and the positive emotions you experience when focusing your thoughts on it. Discuss, too, the negative influences and emotions that are destroying your faith in your ability to actualize it. As a group, help each other debunk the myths and misconceptions that are restricting progress and limiting joy.

CHAPTER 2

GAINING POWER THROUGH YOUR INNER CIRCLE

We lie in the lap of immense intelligence, which makes us receivers of its truth and organs of its activity.

—Ralph Waldo Emerson, "Self-Reliance"

ONE reason that so many individuals fail to lay claim to the abundance reserved for them is that they have developed an inferiority complex, an incorrect understanding of themselves as "less than" other people—less capable, less valuable, and thus less deserving. No belief could be further from the truth.

No one human being is greater than another. Along these same lines, one's trajectory in life is not determined by the advantages or disadvantages with which he or she is born. Regardless of skill set, knowledge, upbringing, and financial status, any individual can achieve success—if they will create an environment that enhances their potential.

RECONCEPTUALIZING EDUCATION

Some individuals with an inferiority complex use a lack of formal education as an alibi for their aimlessness. But as Hill often points out, the sort of knowledge conferred in schools—*general knowledge*—is not particularly helpful for creating success. Only *specialized knowledge*—knowledge that is organized and directed toward a definite end—becomes power, and it can be acquired through means outside of formal schooling. Hill lists five primary sources of specialized knowledge:

1. Personal experience and past formal education

2. The experience and education of others (your mastermind group)

3. Colleges and universities

4. Public libraries

5. Special training courses[29]

Degrees alone "represent nothing but miscellaneous knowledge," but if specialized knowledge is required to live out your definite major purpose, then you can search the venues of knowledge listed above for reliable information.[30] In order to increase your specialized knowledge, Hill recommends the following steps:

1. Identify the gaps in your knowledge.

2. Determine the purpose for which you want the knowledge.

3. Discover where it can be obtained from reliable sources.[31]

Supplementing your knowledge through these means can boost your self-confidence, encouraging you to raise your head high enough for opportunity to see and recognize you. Moreover, when you commit to developing your mental resources through continual personal growth and study, you can resist the temptation to become complacent within your plateaus and find the motivation to keep progressing up the ladder toward success.

Because knowledge is readily available from places other than simply formal institutions of learning, people should never feel limited by not having a certain degree or certification. A truly educated person, Hill says, "is one who has so developed the faculties of his mind that he may acquire anything he wants, or its equivalent, without violating the rights of others."[32] Recognize that whatever knowledge you lack you can obtain through alternate means. As Hill confirms, "Any man is educated who knows where to get knowledge when he needs it, and how to organize that knowledge into definite plans of action."[33]

Education isn't about what you know; it's about being able to locate what you need to know when you need to know it.

Education isn't about what you know; it's about being able to locate what you need to know when you need to know it.

STRENGTH IN NUMBERS: THE MASTERMIND PRINCIPLE

Along with consulting additional venues of specialized knowledge, you can use the mastermind principle to dismantle an inferiority complex resulting from a lack of formal education or a gap in expertise. This principle states that "organized effort is produced through the coordination of effort of two or more people, who work toward a definite end, in a spirit of harmony."[34] Power is simply organized knowledge and coordinated effort, two characteristics of a mastermind group. By allying yourself with individuals whose specialized knowledge complements—not

GAINING POWER THROUGH YOUR INNER CIRCLE

replicates—your own, you can boost your power and increase your self-confidence. For as Hill states, "Men take on the nature and the habits and the POWER OF THOUGHT of those with whom they associate in a spirit of sympathy and harmony."[35]

Henry Ford knew the value of the mastermind principle. He had less than a sixth-grade education, and yet no one today would dare question his intelligence or capability. But in 1916, his knowledge was literally put on trial. A Chicago newspaper labeled him an "ignorant pacifist" in an editorial, and in response, Ford sued the newspaper for libel. During the trial, he was asked a series of history questions in an attempt to prove his ignorance—many of which he could not answer. Growing irritated with the irrelevance of the line of questioning, Ford declared that with one phone call, he would be able to find the answer to any question they could ask him, because he had business associates and allies who could provide information that extended beyond the scope of his expertise.

Ford felt no shame about the gaps in his knowledge; instead, he viewed them as strengths. His laser-like focus on the information most necessary for his pursuits prevented him from cluttering his mind with knowledge that he could find elsewhere. As long as he knew exactly where he could obtain the information he needed right when he needed it, he would never be held back by his so-called ignorance. According to Hill, "every person in the courtroom realized it was the answer, not of an ignorant man, but of a man of EDUCATION.... Through the assistance of his 'Master Mind' group, Henry Ford had at his command all the specialized knoweldge he needed to enable him to become one of the wealthiest men in America."[36]

Andrew Carnegie likewise understood the benefits of the mastermind principle, citing it as one of his main reasons for success. Although he knew nothing about the technical side of the steel business—and what is more, he did not want to know anything about it—he gained the specialized knowledge necessary to manufacture and market steel through the members of his mastermind alliance. As is evident from these two examples:

> You should not have an inferiority complex simply because you do not have all the specialized knowledge you might need of the service or merchandise you intend to provide for your fortune. If you need or desire more, you can cultivate it through your mastermind group.[37]

Forming a mastermind group is key to overcoming your weaknesses and enhancing your strengths, increasing your personal power and ability to transmute your desires into reality.

PRUNING THE CRITICS
FROM YOUR INNER CIRCLE

A mastermind group will support you in your professional endeavors, but you also need a supportive network in your personal life. Great attention must be paid to how you construct your inner circle, because this group of individuals profoundly affects your self-confidence. As Hill explains, "The majority of people permit relatives, friends, and the public at large to so influence them that they cannot live their own lives, because they fear criticism."[38] Even those with a positive opinion of themselves are subject to the deleterious effects of naysayers. Hill reasons:

> If every person whom you met today would tell you that you look sick you would have to have a doctor before night. If the next three people you speak to today should tell you that you look sick you would begin to feel sick.
>
> On the other hand, if every person you see today should tell you what a likeable person you are it would influence you to believe in yourself. If your employer should compliment you each day and tell you what fine work you are doing it would cause you to believe in yourself. If your fellow-workmen should tell you each day that you are doing better

work this would make you have greater confidence in yourself.[39]

As with those thoughts we intentionally plant in our subconscious mind, the thoughts we pick up from our environment embed themselves in our psyche, damaging our sense of self. As will be explored further in the fifth chapter, this process begins in childhood, when we are instructed by family members and close relations to cultivate not self-reliance, but fears and limitations. According to Hill, "Too many people refuse to set high goals for themselves, or even neglect selecting a career, because they fear the criticism of relatives and 'friends' who may say 'Don't aim so high, people will think you are crazy.'"[40]

Often the criticisms and cautions we receive come from well-meaning individuals, but the motivation matters less than the impact in this instance. We carry the burden of criticism with us into adolescence and adulthood, never taking risks on our dreams because we operate with a failure mindset and fear the ridicule of our friends and loved ones. Internalizing the negativity we are fed from our inner circle, we fulfill others' low expectations of ourselves by accepting mediocrity rather than boldly taking action on our definite major purpose.

Even with the firm foundation of self-worth provided for him by his stepmother, Hill sometimes wrestled with this destructive cycle of low self-confidence and inaction stemming from fear of criticism. As he shares:

"

When Andrew Carnegie suggested that I devote twenty years to the organization of a philosophy of individual achievement my first impulse of thought was fear of what people might say. The suggestion set up a goal for me, far out of proportion to any I have ever conceived. As quick as a flash, my mind began to create alibis and excuses, all of them traceable to the inherent FEAR OF CRITICISM. Something inside of me said, "You can't do it—the job is too big, and requires too much time—what will your relatives think of you?—how will you earn a living?—no one has ever organized a philosophy of success, what right have you to believe you can do it?—who are you, anyway, to aim so high?—remember your humble birth—what do you know about philosophy—people will think you are crazy—(and they did)—why hasn't some other person done this before now?[41]

"

Hill's concerns reveal how a self-consciousness about his humble beginnings in a mountain town in Wise County, Virginia, where illiteracy and insolvency were the norm, combined with a fear of criticism from his inner circle to threaten to destroy his dreams before he took action on them.

Surely we all have experienced a self-defeating inner dialogue similar to this one. At one time or another, we likely have put that same question to ourselves of "Who do you think you are?" when envisioning a life of prosperity. Remembering how our loved ones have reacted negatively or incredulously to our lofty goals, we maintain the status quo and "fall in line" instead of charting a new course to abundance. The fear of criticism from our inner circle is so destructive that it "robs man of his initiative, destroys his power of imagination, limits his individuality, takes away his self-reliance, and does him damage in a hundred other ways."[42] It leads to self-consciousness, lack of poise, a feeble personality, indecisiveness, lack of initiative, lack of ambition, an inferiority complex, and many other ills.

Although we cannot choose our parents, siblings, and, to some degree, our supervisors and co-workers, we can counter their negativity by filtering the information we receive from them and assembling an inner circle that supports us in pursuing our definite chief aim. As with our mastermind group, we should seek out individuals who have a positive mental attitude, do not view defeat as final, and encourage freedom of thought. When we surround ourselves with people who encourage us in our success journey because they have faith in our abilities, our self-confidence multiplies exponentially. For "we all need someone to believe in us and to encourage us."[43]

With the aid of a mastermind group and an uplifting inner circle, we can overcome our inferiority complex and attract greater inspiration and opportunities into our lives. But while the support of others is important, our ultimate success depends on our own faith in our ability to achieve our definite chief aim. As Hill writes: "Believe in yourself if you want others to believe in you. Expect success of yourself if you wish others to expect success of you. The world accepts you at pretty much your own valuation, therefore set the value high."[44]

KEY POINTS

No human being is more deserving of success or happiness than another.

An inferiority complex is like a tarnished mirror: wipe away the grime and you can see yourself as you really are. Recognize that you are not defined by...

✓ your upbringing

✓ your education

✓ your expertise

Any individual can achieve success if they create an environment that enhances their potential. The two primary means of supporting personal and professional growth are (1) engaging in continued reading and training and (2) refining your inner circle (both your mastermind group and your close personal associations).

General knowledge, or book learning, does not automatically contribute to success. Only **specialized knowledge**, or knowledge that is organized and directed toward a definite end, becomes power. There are five primary sources for acquiring specialized knowledge:

✓ personal experience and past formal education

✓ the experience and education of others (your mastermind group)

✓ colleges and universities

✓ public libraries

✓ special training courses

🔑 Education is not about what you know; it's about being able to locate what you need to know when you need to know it. Increase your specialized knowledge by...

✓ identifying the gaps in your knowledge

✓ determining the purpose for which you want the knowledge

✓ discovering where it can be obtained from reliable sources

🔑 Create a mastermind group by inviting individuals whose skills, knowledge, and experience complement—not replicate—your own, who encourage freedom of thought, and who do not accept temporary defeat as final.

🔑 Do what you can to eliminate critics and naysayers from your inner circle. Even jokes can plant destructive thoughts in our subconscious mind that bear the fruit of low self-confidence.

🔑 The support of others is important, but the most critical element is belief in yourself. The world will expect greatness from you only when you anticipate greatness for yourself.

🔑 A supportive network and specialized knowledge will be yours when you...

CULTIVATE A STATE OF MIND
TO GAIN POWER

If you have an inferiority complex, examine yourself to identify your perceived weaknesses. Reflect on whether you are truly deficient in these areas, and if you are, make a plan to increase your specialized knowledge using the steps outlined above.

Assess the quality of support you are receiving from the different layers of your inner circle. If you have a mastermind group, do you need to expand or refine it to support your growth? If you do not have a mastermind group, use your response to the question above to identify potential members and invite them to participate. Be prepared to share your own expertise in return for their assistance. Among your family members, friends, and colleagues, are there any individuals whose negativity diminishes your faith in yourself? For those who can be removed from your inner circle, consider spending less time together. For those with whom you must interact, like family members and co-workers, determine how you can filter and redirect their negative energy.

In the context of a study group, share your plans for acquiring specialized knowledge and building a supportive network. Exchange recommendations for additional means of obtaining power through the channels identified in this chapter.

CHAPTER 3

CONDITIONING YOUR MIND
TO RECOGNIZE OPPORTUNITY

Everything lies with yourself. Nothing can keep you down if only you decide that you will move up.

—**Napoleon Hill**, Road to Success

WHILE we cannot completely control the tenor of our environment, we can determine the effect it has on our attitude and sense of self. Accordingly, one of the most important things we can do to ensure our success in life is to continuously build our self-confidence. After all, "opportunities will not come to you unless you have an opinion of yourself big enough to grasp them."[45]

Self-confidence also holds the key to our ability to persevere during challenging times. Hill reveals that "failure is a man-made circumstance. It is never real until it has been accepted by man as permanent. Stating it another way, failure is a state of mind, therefore it is something an individual can control until he neglects to exercise this privilege."[46] The state of mind antithetical to failure is self-confidence. As Carnegie tells Hill, "Confidence is a state of mind, necessary to succeed, and the starting point of developing self-confidence is definiteness of purpose."[47] This chapter provides specific strategies for cultivating a strong sense of self-worth so that you can better recognize opportunity and enhance your resilience.

TAKE PRIDE IN YOUR PURPOSE AND PERFORMANCE

To boost your self-confidence, you should first take inventory of your strengths and contributions and remind yourself of your inherent value. As Hill instructs us:

> Don't pity yourself. Don't lessen your own value in your own eyes. Have confidence in yourself. You are the most important person in the world. You can be what you want to be. Nobody can do so much for you as you can do for yourself. Everything lies with You.[48]

Regardless of whether the work you are currently performing is praiseworthy in the eyes of the world or is the sort you envisioned yourself doing, as long as you are not violating the rights of others you should find reasons to take pride in it.

> The whole of a man's power lies within himself, and a man's first duty is to himself. In carrying out that duty faithfully, you cannot fail to leave your impress on the society in which you move, you cannot fail to raise the standard of your environment, and to dignify all your surroundings.
>
> You may be only one of hundreds or thousands all working in a great business house. Your immediate duties may seem monotonous and trivial. There is no apparent incentive for enthusiasm or personal pride. Be yourself and show yourself. Your job will always be what you want it to be—it will always be what you deserve. It is not your job, it is not your pay, or your conditions, or your prospects—it is YOU.[49]

Perform your job duties diligently and enthusiastically, recognizing that small efforts compound to create large results over time. Display pride in your job by devoting your full attention to it and investing care into your self-presentation. Note that this is not an invitation to become complacent and never attempt to raise your position; it is a directive to give each position, regardless of its desirability, all the energy and effort you can.

> The world is calling for persons who think well of themselves, sufficiently well to dignify themselves by doing each task efficiently.... There is a position waiting for you, but you must show yourself worthy of it by filling your present job so full that your ability shows itself to be running over. Somebody will see it, and use it.[50]

Opportunities will not come to you unless you have an opinion of yourself big enough to grasp them.

Look at the example set by Edwin C. Barnes, a man with little means and no connections who had a burning desire to become Thomas Edison's business associate. Lacking the financial resources even to travel by railroad to Edison's laboratory in Orange, New Jersey, Barnes journeyed there on a freight train and declared his intention to work with the renowned inventor. Impressed with Barnes's resolve, Edison hired him, but not as a business associate; rather, Edison gave him a menial job, which would have discouraged the average individual. Not Barnes— he approached the job as a chance to showcase and develop his strengths. And when the opportunity presented itself to offer his services as a salesman for a new office device that others felt would be difficult to sell, Barnes seized it. He was so successful at selling the device that Edison invited him into a partnership to distribute and market it across the country. Just like Barnes increased his self-confidence through an entry-level position, anyone who takes pleasure and pride in their work and continually seeks to add value to it will find success nearby.

BUILD FAITH THROUGH THE LAW OF AUTOSUGGESTION

As we "go the extra mile" in our current position, finding value in ourselves in and beyond our job, we also must condition our mind to maintain a state of faith. After all, "we are what we are, because of the vibrations of thought which we pick up and register, through the stimuli of our daily environment."[51] By controlling which stimuli reach our subconscious mind, protecting it from destructive thoughts, we enable the principle of autosuggestion to take effect, prompting the subconscious mind to find practical plans for translating our primary desire into reality.

Self-confidence and faith are thus inextricably intertwined: you must believe in your value and capability in order to recognize not only the feasibility, but the *certainty* of your success; what you lack are merely the proper plans to attain your definite chief aim. This interrelationship explains why Hill provides not a recipe for faith, but a formula for self-confidence.

SELF-CONFIDENCE FORMULA

First. I know that I have the ability to achieve the object of my Definite Purpose in life, therefore, I DEMAND of myself persistent, continuous action toward its attainment, and I here and now promise to render such action.

Second. I realize the dominating thoughts of my mind will eventually reproduce themselves in outward, physical action, and gradually transform themselves into physical reality, therefore, I will concentrate my thoughts for thirty minutes daily, upon the task of thinking of the person I intend to become, thereby creating in my mind a clear mental picture of that person.

Third. I know through the principle of auto-suggestion, any desire that I persistently hold in my mind will eventually seek expression through some practical means of attaining the object back of it, therefore, I will devote ten minutes daily to demanding of myself the development of SELF-CONFIDENCE.

Fourth. I have clearly written down a description of my DEFINITE CHIEF AIM in life, and I will never strop trying, until I shall have developed suffi-cient self-confidence for its attainment.

Fifth. I fully realize that no wealth or position can long endure, unless built upon truth and justice, therefore, I will engage in no transaction which does not benefit all whom it affects. I will succeed by attracting to myself the forces I wish to use, and the cooperation of other people. I will induce others to serve me, because of my willingness to serve others. I will eliminate hatred, envy, jealousy, selfishness, and cynicism, by developing love for all humanity, because I know that a negative attitude toward oth-ers can never bring me success. I will cause others to believe in me, because I will believe in them, and in myself.

I will sign my name to this formula, commit it to memory, and repeat it aloud once a day, with full FAITH that it will gradually influence my THOUGHTS and ACTIONS so that I will become a self-reliant, and successful person.[52]

Applying this formula every day will enable you to visualize with increasing clarity what it will be like to achieve your definite major purpose. The more vivid this mental image becomes, the stronger your self-confidence will be, which, in turn, will better enable you to identify advantages that might go otherwise unnoticed.

> Without boosting your self-confidence, you may not recognize or even ignore a plan that is brought to your attention. But with this formula, when an opportunity arises your conscious mind is alerted to what your unconscious mind has been conditioned to discover.[53]

It is a matter of combining the principle of autosuggestion with the principle of concentration. Intense focus on your definite chief aim prompts the principle of autosuggestion to work on the subconscious mind, which uses the mental image as a blueprint for its processes. An earlier version of the Self-Confidence Formula, deriving from Hill's 1917 lectures, recommends not only writing it down and speaking the words aloud, but also employing the aid of a mirror to enhance the effects of your concentration:

> LOOK YOURSELF SQUARELY IN THE EYES, AS THOUGH YOU WERE SOME OTHER PERSON, AND TALK WITH VEHEMENCE! If there is any feeling of lack of courage, shake your fist in the face of that person you see in the glass and make him feel ashamed of himself.
>
> Soon you will actually see the lines on your face begin to change from an expression of weakness to one of strength! You will commence to see strength and beauty in that face which you never saw before, and this wonderful transformation will be quite as noticeable to others.[54]

With the power of autosuggestion on your side, you will soon become the person you intend to be, while not diminishing the value of the person you are right now.

Supplementing the Self-Confidence Formula with daily, positive affirmations can strengthen the mind's resilience against self-doubt.

"

Once these affirmations become habitual and strongly rooted in our subconscious minds, we can call on them at will to strengthen us and to protect us against anything that may sap our self-confidence. Many times just by recalling a time in your past wherein you were exemplary in your approach to an issue or acted in a powerful way, you can call up that very same emotional feeling and relive it in order to produce another positive outcome.[55]

"

By combining definiteness of purpose, a positive mental attitude, faith, autosuggestion, and concentration to cultivate a perpetual mental state of self-confidence, you will give yourself a tremendous advantage in all your endeavors, making failure next to impossible.

KEY POINTS

Self-confidence is antithetical to failure. As Andrew Carnegie defines it for Hill, "Confidence is a state of mind, necessary to succeed, and the starting point of developing self-confidence is definiteness of purpose."

Boost your self-confidence so that you can better recognize opportunity by...

- ✓ taking inventory of your strengths and contributions
- ✓ investing care into your self-presentation
- ✓ going the extra mile
- ✓ conditioning your mind to maintain a state of faith

Regularly visualize the experience of attaining your definite chief aim. The more vivid your mental picture, the stronger your faith will be, which will enhance the likelihood of your success.

Progress and resilience will be yours when you...

CULTIVATE A STATE OF MIND
TO RECOGNIZE OPPORTUNITY

🔑 Create an inventory of your strengths and contributions—
write down at least ten. If you struggle to identify this
many, ask those in your inner circle to help pinpoint
additional positive qualities. Look over your list on a
daily basis to remind yourself of your value.

🔑 Utilize the Self-Confidence Formula reprinted in this
chapter for developing and enhancing your self-
confidence. Repeat it out loud once a day with full faith
that it will progressively influence your thoughts and
actions until you attain your definite chief aim.

🔑 The following is a good creed for you to sign and place
before you at your work, where you can see it each day
and where others can see it. You may find it hard to live
up to this creed at first, but everything worth having
costs a price of some sort. The price of Self-Confidence
is conscientious effort to live up to this creed.[56]

I believe in myself. I believe in those who work with
me. I believe in my employer. I believe in my friends.
I believe in my family. I believe that God will lend me
everything I need with which to succeed if I do my best
to earn it through faithful, efficient and honest service.
I believe in prayer and I will never close my eyes in
sleep without praying for Divine guidance to the end

that I will be patient with other people and tolerant with those who do not think as I do. I believe that success is the result of intelligent effort and does not depend upon luck, sharp practices or double-crossing friends, fellow-workmen or my employer. I believe that I will get out of life exactly what I put into it, therefore I will be careful to conduct myself toward others as I would be willing to have them act toward me. I will not slander those whom I do not like, I will not slight my work no matter what I may see others doing. I will render the best service that is in me because I have pledged myself to succeed in life and I know that success is always the result of conscientious effort. Finally, I will forgive those who offend me because I realize that I will sometimes offend others and I will need their forgiveness.

_____

(Signed)

 In the context of a study group, brainstorm and discuss ways that you can go the extra mile in your career. Describe current projects on which you're working, and invite group members to provide insight on possible opportunities for advancement.

CHAPTER 4

BUILDING FAITH THROUGH ACTION

Do the thing and you shall have the power.

—Ralph Waldo Emerson, "Compensation"

O NCE you have expanded your power through your master-mind alliance and personal network and conditioned your mind to operate in a state of faith, you encounter the most crucial component to developing self-confidence: *action*. The nature of your thoughts matters little unless they take shape as organized plans and solidify into actions. Through action, you can eradicate the fears and self-doubt that threaten to diminish your self-confidence and enhance your self-worth. It is in boldly taking action on your definite chief aim that you will discover the unquenchable force within the core of your being, the potency of your efforts, and your ability to overcome obstacles.

During their 1908 interview, Andrew Carnegie shared with Hill that self-confidence was one of the most crucial ingredients to success. As he explained to Hill, no obstacle or disadvantage—poverty, lack of education, absent support network—could stand in the way of someone with a strong sense of self-worth. Accordingly, the cardinal rule of Carnegie's philosophy of personal achievement was to develop one's self-confidence by taking action on a definite plan for achievement. He asserts:

> The man who knows exactly what he wants, has a definite plan for getting it, and is actually engaged in carrying out his plan will soon believe he has the ability in himself to succeed. The man who procrastinates soon loses confidence and does little or nothing worthwhile.[57]

Action prevents drifting, which draws individuals down the road to insecurity and self-loathing. We feel good about ourselves when we are pursuing a noble aim. Progress is truly invigorating. With each milestone we reach along our success journey, we experience a renewed sense of pride and satisfaction. As we celebrate our victories, we become more secure in our purpose— more sure of who we are meant to be. It is therefore crucial that we learn to apply our power through action.

Progress is truly invigorating.

TAKE ACTION AND FAITH WILL FOLLOW

Inaction weakens our resolve, depletes our creative powers, and predisposes us to second-guessing ourselves. This is because "indecision crystallizes into DOUBT" and "the two blend and become FEAR!"[58] Decisiveness, in contrast, boosts our self-confidence and elevates our mind to a higher plane of functioning, whereby our thoughts are more apt to attract inspiration and opportunity. As Hill explains:

> Those who reach DECISIONS promptly and definitely, know what they want, and generally get it. The leaders in every walk of life DECIDE quickly, and firmly. That is the major reason why they are leaders. The world has a habit of making room for the man whose words and actions show that he knows where he is going.[59]

The story of Dr. Frank W. Gunsaulus provides an excellent case study of the relationship between decisiveness, action, and self-confidence. A young clergyman, Dr. Gunsaulus possessed a burning desire to found an educational institution that privileged experiential learning. However, he faced the obstacle of raising a million dollars to carry out his plans. Day in and day out for two years, he mulled over options for accumulating the funds necessary for his project, until one day he realized that he had to move beyond thought into action. He recounts how his decision to act boosted his self-confidence:

> The moment I reached a definite decision to get the money within a specified time, a strange feeling of assurance came over me, such as I had never before experienced. Something inside me seemed to say, "Why didn't you reach that decision a long time ago? The money was waiting for you all the time!"[60]

Once he decided on a definite time by which he would obtain the money, Dr. Gunsaulus quickly found inspiration for the plans to accomplish this task. He contacted the newspapers to inform them that he would be preaching a sermon the next day on "What I would do if I had a Million Dollars." Because founding such an educational institution was his burning desire—the definite major purpose on which all of his thoughts were focused—he had no problem drafting the sermon; he had been rehearsing it in his mind for the past two years. He confidently prayed that someone in the audience would be moved to provide the necessary amount. With full assurance that his prayer would be heard, Dr. Gunsaulus delivered a powerful speech that detailed his plans for organizing a school where students would acquire practical knowledge while also learning how to develop their minds. As soon as he concluded his sermon and took his seat, Dr. Gunsaulus was approached by a man named Phillip D. Armour, who invited Dr. Gunsaulus to come to his office the next day to receive the one million dollars he needed to found his educational institution. And thus was born the Armour Institute of Technology.

Sometimes we hesitate to act because we are uncertain of our success. However, delaying taking action on our goals until we reach some artificially determined threshold of capability ensures that we will become increasingly less able to reach them, for our resolve and faith will weaken even as our knowledge grows.

The joy of self-reliance becomes the "stickability" of self-confidence.

The question now arises as to whether *all* action leads to self-confidence, for would not efforts that end in defeat deal our ego a blow? Hill posed this same question to Carnegie, who responded with the following proclaimation: "Every failure carries within it the seed of an equivalent benefit. Great leaders' lives show that their success is in proportion to their mastery of temporary defeat."[61] As we will explore further in the next chapter, the ultimate self-confidence derives from learning how to navigate uncertain or difficult situations on one's own. When we persevere through the challenges that life presents us, we cultivate an unshakeable belief in ourselves.

DISCOVER POWER BY GOING THE EXTRA MILE

In order to convert our actions into power, we must pair decisiveness with enthusiasm—positive energy that motivates us to "go the extra mile." Hill's success philosophy leaves no room for self-pity or negativity about one's circumstances. For "to become despondent about your lot in life is but to belittle yourself. To be determined on better things, and ready and anxious to work for better things, will surely bring its reward."[62]

As the preface mentions, Hill originally considered self-confidence to be the first "requisite" for success, but it later became grouped under the banner of "enthusiasm." The two states are certainly interrelated, as enthusiasm is "that great dynamic force which puts self-confidence into action."[63] When we cultivate the state of mind of self-confidence, our thoughts are emotionalized by enthusiasm. This, in turn, magnifies the power of autosuggestion to work on our subconscious mind, helping us create and implement definite plans.

Enthusiasm is so stimulating that it improves our personal initiative, motivating us to perform our duties and actions at a higher level than is expected, which feeds back into our enthusiasm. This constructive, self-perpetuating loop of self-confidence ensures that we are continually magnifying our power by augmenting our thoughts and actions with faith and enthusiasm. As Hill explains, "This business of going the extra mile and making it your business to take pleasure out of going the extra mile certainly does develop personal initiative. It causes you to get joy out of acting on your own initiative."[64] The joy of self-reliance becomes the "stickability" of self-confidence. Nothing will stand in the way of individuals who enthusiastically commit themselves wholeheartedly to finding ways to add value in all their endeavors.

"Lincoln started in a log hut and stopped in the White House—because he believed in himself. Napoleon began as a poor Corsican and brought half of Europe to his feet—because he believed in himself. Henry Ford started as a poor farmer lad and put more wheels into motion than any other man on earth—because he believed in himself. Rockefeller started as a poor bookkeeper and became the world's richest man—because he believed in himself. They took that which they wished because they had confidence in their own ability. Now, the question is, WHY DO YOU NOT DECIDE WHAT YOU WANT, THEN GO OUT AND TAKE IT?[65]"

KEY POINTS

Thought must be followed by action. It is through decisive action that we can eradicate the fears and self-doubt that threaten to diminish our self-confidence.

Inaction weakens our resolve, depletes our creative powers, and predisposes us to second-guessing ourselves.

When we make progress toward achieving our chief desire, we gain momentum, which renews our pride and satisfaction and builds self-confidence.

Don't wait to take action on your dreams until you feel prepared for success—your resolve and faith will weaken in the interim. Obstacles will contain opportunities for growth and achievement.

Pair decisiveness with enthusiasm—positive energy that motivates you to go the extra mile.

Enthusiasm and personal initiative will be yours when you...

CULTIVATE A STATE OF MIND
TO TAKE DECISIVE ACTION

🔑 Repeat the five steps in the Self-Confidence Formula outlined in the previous chapter in a state of mind of enthusiasm. In other words, while holding your definite chief aim in your mind, emotionalize your mental picture by attaching enthusiasm to it. Discover the motivation this provides for going the extra mile.

🔑 In the context of a study group, discuss decisions on which you have been wavering that are related to your definite major purpose. What has been holding you back from taking action? Can you identify where your hesitancy is coming from? Determine one action you could take this week to create positive change in your life.

CHAPTER 5

INSTILLING SELF-CONFIDENCE

IN THE NEXT GENERATION

We can accomplish much when we learn to expect much of ourselves.

—**Napoleon Hill,** "Opportunity"

WITH each generation growing increasingly lean in self-confidence, it is crucial that we focus on developing not only our own self-worth, but also the self-worth of today's youth. If you ask an experienced educator what the number one cause of misbehavior and poor performance in school is, they will undoubtedly answer: *low self-esteem.* We may not be able to control children's environment, where bullying and toxic media can diminish self-confidence during the most formative years, but we can build their self-confidence through direct intervention. For parents, family members, mentors, caretakers, teachers and others who spend time with children, this means, first and foremost, avoiding criticism and focusing on capability and, second, teaching children the pride that comes from navigating age-appropriate challenges on their own.

AVOID CRITICISM

Criticism has a self-fulfilling function. When you label a child as "naughty" or "bad" or tell them that they will never amount to anything in life, they internalize those words, and their subconscious mind works to materialize the negative thoughts. The subconscious mind is particularly pliant in childhood, so the harsh, unfeeling words of family members and mentors can profoundly impair a child's sense of self, predisposing them to failure consciousness for the rest of their lives. Hill emphasizes that:

> Parents often do their children irreparable injury by criticizing them. The mother of one of my boyhood chums used to punish him with a switch almost daily, always completing the job with the statement, "You'll land in the penitentiary before you are

twenty." He was sent to a Reformatory at the age of seventeen.[66]

Hill knew better than anyone the power of words to lower or raise a child's self-esteem. Born into poverty and illiteracy, he was not expected to achieve anything great in life. He acted in accordance with those expectations, stirring up trouble in his boyhood. But when his father remarried a woman by the name of Martha Ramey Banner a year after his mother died, Hill was quickly scooped off the path to failure and placed firmly on the path to success. Don Green, the executive director and CEO of the Napoleon Hill Foundation, tells the story this way:

At the age of eleven Hill was persuaded by his stepmother to consider becoming a writer because of his unbounded imagination. Martha said to her stepson, "If you would devote as much time to reading and writing as you have to causing trouble, you might live to see the time when your influence will be felt throughout the state."

By the time Hill was twelve, his stepmother had convinced him to trade the gun he was so proud of for a typewriter. This was in 1895, when typewriters were not readily available. Martha again encouraged the often mischevious boy, telling him, "If you become as good with a typewriter as you are with that gun, you may become rich and famous and known throughout the world."[67]

Of course we know how the seed of thought planted by Hill's stepmother flourished, giving Hill the self-confidence to work tirelessly for decades to make the first comprehensive success philosophy available to the general public and to persevere through a number of business failures over the course of his life.

Parents, close relations, educators, and mentors should take note of the significant influence they have on the children in their life. As children form their sense of self, they require validation from adults in order to become confident enough in who they are to pursue their definite major purpose. They need someone who will foster their sense of individuality, sharing advice like that from Emerson:

Insist on yourself; never imitate. Your own gift you can present every moment with the cumulative force of a whole life's cultivation; but of the adopted talent of another, you have only an extemporaneous, half possession.[68]

While children certainly can overcome their childhood programming later in life, they are much more likely to succeed and enjoy a fulfilling existence if they operate from a state of self-confidence. Planting the seeds of fear, resentment, hatred, bitterness, and poverty consciousness, criticism sprouts into limiting beliefs and codependent behaviors that can be difficult to uproot.

GROW A CHILD'S MENTAL GARDEN

Instead of receiving a daily education in their faults and foibles, children should be taught their inherent capability—their power to create the life of their dreams by controlling their thoughts. Most any child can appreciate the basic principles of Hill's success philosophy.

If children can memorize and recite nursery rhymes that stay with them for a lifetime, they can easily learn to program their subconscious minds for success using the same memory tools. Affirmations, self-confidence formulas, action plans, and commands such as "Do it now!" assist those of us who are convinced that these techniques predispose us to positive outcomes.

Share these secrets with young people who are ready to begin their life's gardens. You can be the master gardener who sets the vision for a positive life outcome just by using the gardening metaphor. Life can be a garden. Life began in a garden. Why not demonstrate to a child how to use the tools they have been given to grow their life's garden exactly to their specifications?[69]

Set children on the path to success by providing them with memory tools to cultivate their success consciousness. You will be amazed at how planting the seeds of self-confidence early in life will yield a garden of abundance later on.

INSPIRE SELF-RELIANCE

In addition to teaching children to harness the power of their thoughts using affirmations and action plans, we must give them the greatest gift and most crucial foundation for success—*self-reliance*. So many children are hindered by their parents' overzealousness to protect them from any source of discouragement. Young people need to experience the frustration that comes with figuring things out on their own. If their parents or loved ones always step in to fix their problems before they have a chance to work through them, they will feel inadequate and become dependent on others to solve all their difficulties.

> Give children the greatest gift and most crucial foundation for success—*self-reliance*.

On the other hand, giving children the space to err and rebound—to navigate temporary defeat and discover the opportunities that emerge from within obstacles—enables them to become poised, resolute, self-sufficient individuals who can think for themselves. When children realize that they can use their own mental resources to navigate uncertainties and difficulties in life, they develop a firm confidence in their abilities that makes them strong leaders and high achievers later in life. As Hill says, "Necessity is a teacher of great sagacity."[70] Discovering one's resourcefulness is so critical to developing self-confidence that Hill explains:

"

My first task in advising people who lack self-confidence is to save them from themselves. Figuratively speaking, they must be taken out into the field and allowed to "run away," just as a horse might do. They must discover their real strength. They must learn that their weakness exists nowhere except in their own deceptive imaginations.[71]

"

Let children discover their power through play, without hovering and preventing anything from causing them even momentary discomfort. The creativity and resolve that they will gain through trial-and-error learning will build up their self-worth and save them from the modern malady of helplessness. This is a great calling, one to which all those with influence over children's lives should heed. As Hill proclaims:

"

With all these great lessons which we have learned we stand face to face, now, with the opportunity to impose the sum total of what we have learned upon the minds of our children so that it may become a part of their philosophy and lead the next generation to heights of attainment that will startle the world.

This is the only method through which we can pass on to posterity the benefit of that which we have learned through combat, struggle and experimentation. What a glorious opportunity now awaits the leadership of men and women in the Schools, Churches and Public Press, the three leading mediums through which these great lessons can be firmly planted in the minds of our young.

[...]

Let us all contribute our individual support and co-operation to the end that our children may be taught the advantages of placing principle above the dollar and humanity, as a whole, above the individual.[72]

"

KEY POINTS

- Low self-esteem is a major—if not the primary—cause of children's misbehavior and poor academic performance.

- Parents, caretakers, family members, teachers, mentors, and others can build children's self-confidence by...

  - ✓ avoiding criticism

  - ✓ highlighting capability

  - ✓ instilling self-reliance

- Criticism has a self-fulfilling function: children internalize when adults call them "naughty" or "bad" or tell them that they will never amount to much, and then their subconscious mind works to materialize those negative thoughts.

- Grow a child's mental garden by sowing the seeds of self-worth. Use affirmations, self-confidence formulas, action plans, and other tools of encouragement in a manner like nursery rhymes: memorization and recitation of positive statements will yield self-confidence and success consciousness.

- Foster children's sense of individuality and encourage their ability to problem-solve. Allow room for children to experience the frustration of figuring out how to overcome age-appropriate obstacles, and you will give them an invaluable gift: *self-reliance*.

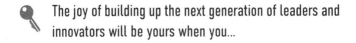

The joy of building up the next generation of leaders and innovators will be yours when you...

CULTIVATE A STATE OF MIND
TO INSPIRE
SELF-CONFIDENCE IN OTHERS

Encourage children to recite Edgar Albert Guest's poem "It Couldn't Be Done." Through the pleasure of rhyme and rhythm, it will help children remember to have faith in themselves and to persist in their efforts to attain their definite major purpose.

If you have young children, use craft time to create affirmations that you can hang up in their room. Make it fun: color them, add stickers, or decorate them in a way that makes them appealing to young eyes. If your children are older, give them a journal and provide them with prompts that incite self-exploration to help them discover, and solidify their confidence in, their strengths. Share books that inspire personal growth, and carve out regular study sessions to exchange thoughts on the readings.

Create a small, age-appropriate problem for a child to solve. For example, present a toddler with a take-apart toy whose parts have been disconnected, and invite them to piece it back together. (For older children, find more age-appropriate tasks—of course, nothing dangerous or overly difficult, just something to help them develop their critical thinking skills such as a hypothetical scenario to consider.) Restrain yourself from stepping in to help; acknowledge and validate their attempts, and encourage them to persist in their efforts. Once they accomplish that task, present them with a slightly more challenging one. By scaffolding problem-solving opportunities, children will grow their practical wisdom, their self-reliance, and their self-confidence simultaneously.

 In the context of a study group, discuss strategies for supporting children in enlarging their self-confidence. Identify opportunities for mentorship and positively influencing children whose self-confidence was stunted earlier in life.

HOW TO DEVELOP SELF-CONFIDENCE

BY NAPOLEON HILL

"Selling yourself short is effrontery to your Creator."

THE greatest person now living is the one who is reading this sentence. If you do not recognize this truth, then you should begin at once to follow these instructions:

- Adopt a Definite Major Purpose and begin where you stand to attain it.

- Write out a clear statement of what you believe to be the advantages of your Definite Major Purpose, and call these into your mind many times daily, in the form of a prayer for attainment.

- If your Major Purpose is to attain something material, such as money, see yourself already in possession of it when you call it into your consciousness.

- Associate yourself with as many people as possible who are in sympathy with you and your Major Purpose, and induce them to give you encouragement and faith in every way possible.

- Let not a single day pass without making at least one move toward the attainment of your Definite Major Purpose, and remember that nothing worthwhile is ever accomplished without ACTION—ACTION—ACTION!

- Choose some prosperous, self-reliant person as your "pace-maker" and make up your mind not only to catch up with him in achievements, but to excel him.

- When you meet with defeat, when obstacles get in your way and the going is hard, do not quit, but turn on more will power and keep on keeping on.

- Follow the habit of never running away from disagreeable circumstances, but learn to transmute them into inspiration for the achievement of your desires.

- And remember that LOVE and Hate had a falling out. Hate drew a ring around himself that shut LOVE out, but LOVE got busy with a great big grin and drew a bigger ring that took Hate and his little ring in again.

- Lastly, recognize the truth that everything worth having has a price one must pay to get it. The price of self-

HOW TO DEVELOP SELF-CONFIDENCE

confidence is eternal vigilance in carrying out these instructions. Your watchword must be PERSISTENCY.

And remember, if you sell yourself short through lack of self-confidence you thereby express ingratitude to your Creator, whose one and only exclusive privilege to you is that of mastering and using your own mind for the determination of your own earthly destiny.

Journal

_____

_____

_____

_____

_____

_____

_____

_____

_____

_____

_____

_____

_____

_____

_____

_____

_____

_____

_____

_____

_____

_____

_____

_____

_____

_____

_____

JOURNAL

SELF-CONFIDENCE FORMULA

98

JOURNAL

JOURNAL

NOTES

1. Napoleon Hill, "Self-Confidence," lecture delivered in "Applied Psychology," George Washington Institute, Chicago, IL, 1917, D1.

2. Napoleon Hill, *Outwitting the Devil* (Shippensburg, PA: Sound Wisdom, 2020), 20–21.

3. Andrew Carnegie quoted in Napoleon Hill, *Napoleon Hill's Greatest Speeches* (Shippensburg, PA: Sound Wisdom, 2016), 20.

4. Hill, *Napoleon Hill's Greatest Speeches* (Shippensburg, PA: Sound Wisdom, 2016), 40.

5. Hill, "Self-Confidence," D5.

6. Napoleon Hill, *Napoleon Hill's Success Principles Rediscovered* (Shippensburg, PA: Sound Wisdom, 2017), 172.

7. Hill, *Greatest Speeches*, 41.

8. Hill, "Self-Confidence," D2.

9. Don M. Green quoted in Hill, *Greatest Speeches*, 11.

10. Napoleon Hill, *Think and Grow Rich* (Shippensburg, PA: Sound Wisdom, 2017), 74–75.

11. Hill, *Greatest Speeches*, 40–41.

12. Napoleon Hill, *Napoleon Hill's Gold Standard* (Shippensburg, PA: Sound Wisdom, 2016), 49.

13. Ralph Waldo Emerson, "Self-Reliance," in *Essays* (New York: Charles E. Merrill Co., 1907), 80, http://www.gutenberg.org/files/16643/16643-h/16643-h.htm#SELF-RELIANCE.

14. Hill, "Self-Confidence," D9.

15. Napoleon Hill and Judith Williamson, *Napoleon Hill's Life Lessons* (Shippensburg, PA: Sound Wisdom, 2008), 29.

16. Hill, "Self-Confidence," D1.

17. William Ernest Henley, "Invictus," http://www.poetryfoundation.org/poems/51642/invictus.

18. Emerson, "Self-Reliance," 81.

19. Hill, *Think and Grow Rich*, 32–33.

20. Emerson, "Self-Reliance," 83.

21. Hill, "Self-Confidence," D15.

22. Napoleon Hill, *The Master-Key to Riches* (1945; repr., Shippensburg, PA: Sound Wisdom, 2018), 168.

23. Hill, "Self-Confidence," D7.

24. The six basic fears are the fear of poverty, the fear of criticism, the fear of ill health, the fear of loss of love, the fear of old age, and the fear of death.

25. Hill, *Think and Grow Rich*, 47.

26. Napoleon Hill, *Think and Grow Rich in Ten Minutes a Day* (Shippensburg, PA: Sound Wisdom, 2020), 67.

27. Hill, *Outwitting the Devil*, 140.

28. Hill, *Think and Grow Rich*, 297.

29. Ibid., 109–10.
30. Ibid., 110.
31. Hill, *Think and Grow Rich in Ten Minutes a Day*, 44.
32. Hill, *Think and Grow Rich*, 106.
33. Ibid., 107.
34. Ibid., 249.
35. Ibid., 254.
36. Ibid., 107.
37. Hill, *Think and Grow Rich in Ten Minutes a Day*, 43.
38. Hill, *Think and Grow Rich*, 236.
39. Napoleon Hill, *Napoleon Hill's Road to Success: The Classic Guide for Prosperity and Happiness* (New York: TarcherPerigee, 2016), 21.
40. Hill, *Think and Grow Rich*, 240.
41. Ibid., 237.
42. Ibid., 342.
43. Hill, *Road to Success*, 21.
44. Ibid., 23.
45. Ibid., 31.
46. Hill, *Outwitting the Devil*, 255.
47. Carnegie quoted in Hill, *Greatest Speeches*, 20.
48. Hill, *Road to Success*, 32.
49. Ibid., 30.
50. Ibid., 31.
51. Hill, *Think and Grow Rich*, 73.
52. Ibid., 74–75.
53. Hill, *Gold Standard*, 202–03.
54. Hill, "Self-Confidence," D8.

55. Hill, *Life Lessons*, 29–30.

56. Hill, *Road to Success*, 27–28.

57. Carnegie quoted in Hill, *Greatest Speeches*, 20.

58. Hill, *Think and Grow Rich*, 327.

59. Ibid., 223.

60. Frank W. Gunsaulus quoted in Hill, *Think and Grow Rich*, 137–38.

61. Carnegie quoted in Hill, *Greatest Speeches*, 20.

62. Hill, *Road to Success*, 30.

63. Hill, *Greatest Speeches*, 43.

64. Ibid., 241.

65. Hill, *Road to Success*, 32.

66. Hill, *Think and Grow Rich*, 342.

67. Don Green quoted in Hill, *Greatest Speeches*, 16.

68. Emerson, "Self-Reliance," 110–11.

69. Hill, *Gold Standard*, 74.

70. Hill, *Outwitting the Devil*, 200.

71. Hill, *Greatest Speeches*, 41.

72. Napoleon Hill, "Opportunity," *Napoleon Hill's Magazine* 1, no. 8 (January 1922). Reprinted in *Napoleon Hill's Success Secrets Rediscovered*, rev. ed. (Shippensburg, PA: Sound Wisdom, 2017), 173.

ABOUT THE AUTHOR

NAPOLEON HILL was born in 1883 in a one-room cabin on the Pound River in Wise County, Virginia. He began his writing career at age 13 as a "mountain reporter" for small town newspapers and went on to become America's most beloved motivational author. Hill passed away in November 1970 after a long and successful career writing, teaching, and lecturing about the principles of success. Dr. Hill's work stands as a monument to individual achievement and is the cornerstone of modern motivation. His book, *Think and Grow Rich,* is the all-time bestseller in the field. Hill established the Foundation as a nonprofit educational institution whose mission is to perpetuate his philosophy of leadership, self-motivation, and individual achievement. His books, audio cassettes, videotapes, and other motivational products are made available to you as a service of the Foundation so that you may build your own library of personal achievement materials...and help you acquire financial wealth and the true riches of life.

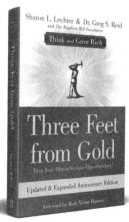  

ADDITIONAL TITLES FROM THE NAPOLEON HILL FOUNDATION

Freedom from Your Fears

Gift of Giving

Law of Success

Magic Ladder to Success

Master-Key to Riches

Napoleon Hill's Action Activities for Health, Wealth and Happiness

Napoleon Hill's Gold Standard

Napoleon Hill's Greatest Speeches

Napoleon Hill's Keys to Personal Achievement

Napoleon Hill's Life Lessons

Napoleon Hill's Positive Thinking

Napoleon Hill's Power of Positive Action

Napoleon Hill's Self-Confidence Formula

Napoleon Hill's Success Principles Rediscovered

Outwitting the Devil

Success and Something Greater

Think and Grow Rich

Think and Grow Rich: The Legacy

Three Feet from Gold

The Law of Success

soundwisdom.com/naphill